GETTING TO KNOW THE WORLD'S GREATEST INVENTORS & SCIENTISTS

D1308693

DANIEL HALE

WILLIAMS

Surgeon Who Opened Hearts and Minds

WRITTEN AND ILLUSTRATED BY MIKE VENEZIA

CHILDREN'S PRESS®

AN IMPRINT OF SCHOLASTIC INC.

NEW YORK   TORONTO   LONDON   AUCKLAND   SYDNEY

MEXICO CITY   NEW DELHI   HONG KONG

DANBURY, CONNECTICUT

Content Consultant: Stephanie Davenport, Ed.D., Director of Educational Services, DuSable Museum of African American History, Chicago

Reading Consultant: Nanci R. Vargus, Ed.D., Assistant Professor, School of Education, University of Indianapolis

Photographs © 2010: Corbis Images/Bettmann: 3, 13; Everett Collection, Inc./Wisconsin Historical Society: 11; Getty Images/Thinkstock: 18; Moorland Spingarn Research Center, Howard University, Washington, D.C.: 6, 8 left, 8 right, 10, 16 top, 27, 29, 31 (Prints and Photographs Department, D.H. Williams Papers); New York Public Library, Astor, Lenox and Tilden Foundations: 20 (General Research & Reference Division, Schomburg Center for Research in Black Culture); Courtesy of Northwestern University, Chicago, IL: 30 (Galter Health Sciences Library Special Collections); Phototake/Nucleus Medical Art, Inc.: 23; Rock County Historical Society: 22 (Original lent by DuSable Museum of African American History, IF252); The Granger Collection, New York: 14; The Image Works/SSPL: 16 bottom.

Colorist for illustrations: Andrew Day

Library of Congress Cataloging-in-Publication Data

Venezia, Mike.
  Daniel Hale Williams : surgeon who opened hearts and minds / written and illustrated by Mike Venezia.
    p. cm. — (Getting to know the world's greatest inventors and scientists)
  Includes index.
  ISBN-13: 978-0-531-23729-8 (lib. bdg.)   978-0-531-22350-5 (pbk.)
  ISBN-10: 0-531-23729-X (lib. bdg.)   0-531-22350-7 (pbk.)
  1. Williams, Daniel Hale, 1856-1931—Juvenile literature. 2. African American surgeons—Biography—Juvenile literature. 3. Surgeons—United States—Biography—Juvenile literature. I. Title.
  RD27.35.W54V564 2010
  617.092—dc22
  [B]
                              2009030221

No part of this publication may be reproduced in whole or in part, or stored in a retrieval system, or transmitted in any form or by any means, electronic, mechanical, photocopying, recording, or otherwise, without written permission of the publisher. For information regarding permission, write to Scholastic Inc., 557 Broadway, New York, NY 10012.

© 2010 by Mike Venezia.

All rights reserved. Published in 2010 by Children's Press, an imprint of Scholastic Inc. Published simultaneously in Canada. Printed in China.

SCHOLASTIC, CHILDREN'S PRESS, and associated logos are trademarks and/or registered trademarks of Scholastic Inc.

2 3 4 5 6 7 8 9 10 R 19 18 17 16 15 14 13 12 11 10   62

Dr. Daniel Hale Williams was a renowned surgeon who founded the first **non-segregated** hospital in the United States. He was also a pioneer in performing surgery on the lining around the heart.

Daniel Hale Williams was born in Hollidaysburg, Pennsylvania, in 1856. An African American, he became a remarkable doctor and surgeon during a time when African Americans faced a great deal of **racial prejudice** in the United States. Slavery had ended in 1865, but black people were still denied many rights and opportunities. Dr. Williams dedicated his life to making sure that African Americans would not only be able to get good medical care, but would also be free to pursue medicine as a career.

Many hospitals at the time refused to admit black patients or gave them inferior treatment. Dr. Williams was determined to change that. In 1891, Dr. Williams founded Provident Hospital, a thirteen-bed hospital in Chicago, Illinois. He helped raise the money to build it, hired doctors, and got people to donate beds and equipment. Provident Hospital treated anyone—black or white—who needed medical help.

A thirteen-bed hospital seems pretty small by today's standards, but in the late 1800s, there

weren't many hospitals around. Doctors usually operated in their offices or on a patient's kitchen or dining room table!

Dr. Williams had another goal in mind in creating Provident Hospital. Most medical schools and nursing schools refused to admit students who were black, and few hospitals would hire black doctors. Dr. Williams wanted to create a place that would accept and give excellent training to black doctors and nurses.

Daniel Hale Williams was born a few years before the Civil War began. One of the main reasons the Civil War was fought was to end slavery in the South. Dan and his family lived in the North, where slavery was illegal, so they were free.

When Dan was growing up, Hollidaysburg was a busy town. Dan had a happy childhood there.

Daniel Hale Williams at the age of six

Dan's father was a barber. Mr. Williams had plenty of customers and made enough money to give his wife and seven children a comfortable life. Dan helped his dad out by keeping shaving mugs, brushes, razors, and scissors neat and clean. Dan also learned to cut hair at an early age.

Daniel Hale Williams's parents,
Daniel and Sarah Williams

When Dan was eleven years old, a terrible tragedy happened. His father became ill and died unexpectedly. Mrs. Williams couldn't afford to raise her large family alone, and had to split her family up. Some of Dan's sisters went to stay with relatives.

Mrs. Williams took two of her daughters to live in Illinois. Dan ended up becoming an **apprentice** to a shoemaker in Baltimore, Maryland. Dan learned how to make and repair shoes, but he hated the job. It wasn't long before he decided to leave the shoemaker and join his mom in Rockford, Illinois.

In Rockford, Dan became a barber's apprentice. Then, as a teenager, he moved to Wisconsin to be near his sister and attend high school. To support himself, he opened up his own barbershop. Even though he owned the shop, Dan didn't make very much money. He was happy to be offered a job in the nearby town of Janesville. At the age of seventeen, Dan went to work for Harry Anderson, who owned the largest barbershop in town. Harry really liked Dan and offered him a place to stay for free.

As a teenager, Daniel Hale Williams ran his own barbershop.

Daniel moved to Janesville, Wisconsin (above), when he was seventeen.

Daniel Hale Williams was always a hard worker. Even though he spent long hours every day at the barbershop, he finished high school, and even found time to learn to play the guitar and bass fiddle. Harry Anderson was in a band, and Dan sometimes joined the band and played at dances around the state.

Although Daniel Hale Williams enjoyed being a barber, he felt he could accomplish more. For a while, he studied law, but he didn't find it interesting enough. Then he remembered a man he had met in the barbershop, Dr. Henry Palmer. Daniel admired Dr. Palmer. He was known as a hero in the area. Dr. Palmer would travel through rain or snow in the middle of the night to help save a patient's life, deliver a baby, or set a broken limb.

This 1879 illustration shows a country doctor reading a signpost to help him find his way to a patient in the middle of the night. Daniel Hale Williams was inspired to become a doctor after witnessing the similar dedication of Dr. Henry Palmer.

Daniel liked the idea of helping people. He made an appointment to see Dr. Palmer to discuss the possibility of becoming a doctor someday.

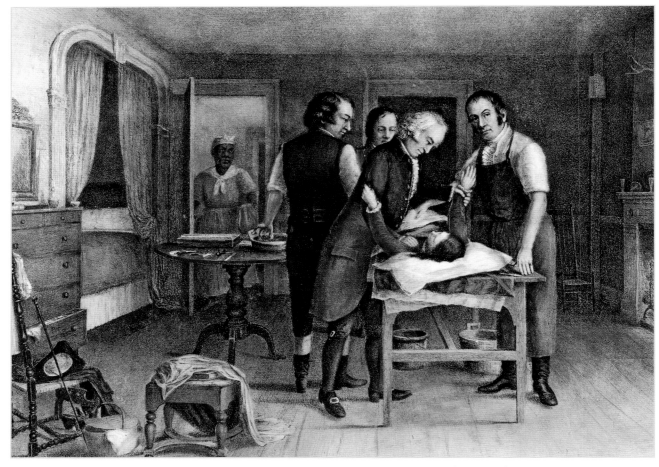

Up until the late 1800s, most surgery was done in the patient's home (above). For two years, Daniel Hale Williams was an assistant to Dr. Palmer, learning all he could about medicine as he accompanied the doctor from house to house.

Dr. Palmer was impressed with Daniel's energy and desire to help people. Eventually, Daniel asked if he could become Dr. Palmer's assistant. Before he considered taking Daniel on, Dr. Palmer went over all the things a local doctor had to do. Many of them were extremely difficult, and even unpleasant.

Daniel didn't care about that, though. He had made up his mind and was ready for the challenge. Dr. Palmer was an excellent teacher. He taught Daniel and two other young assistants how to stitch up wounds, help set broken bones, and deliver babies. They watched Dr. Palmer **amputate** badly injured limbs when it was absolutely necessary.

After two years, Dr. Palmer suggested that Daniel Williams continue his education at the Chicago Medical College (which later became part of Northwestern University Medical School). This school was one of the best medical schools in the country.

Daniel Hale Williams as a medical student

In 1880, Daniel Hale Williams traveled to Chicago, Illinois. He found a place to live, passed the medical school's entrance exam, and began his studies.

Daniel spent three years at the Chicago Medical College. It was an exciting time in medicine. The recent discovery of **anesthesia** helped doctors control a patient's pain and allowed surgeons to do more complicated surgeries deeper inside the body.

These are some of the instruments surgeons used in the mid-1800s.

However, at the time, most surgeons did not yet understand that **bacteria** and other **germs** cause **infection.** Some doctors would probe wounds with unwashed hands or operate while wearing street clothes that weren't **sterile.** This lack of cleanliness caused more patients to die from infections than from their illnesses. Daniel learned about new methods to prevent these needless deaths, such as handwashing, sterilizing equipment, and spraying the patient and operating area with **antiseptics.**

After three years of medical school, Daniel Williams graduated. He was now a full-fledged doctor. Although he had been the only African American student in his class, he hadn't experienced prejudice while in medical school. When he began looking for a job, however, he ran into problems. No Chicago city hospital would accept a black doctor on its staff. So Dr. Williams decided to open his own practice. He continued to improve his surgical skills and learned better ways to reduce the risks of infection.

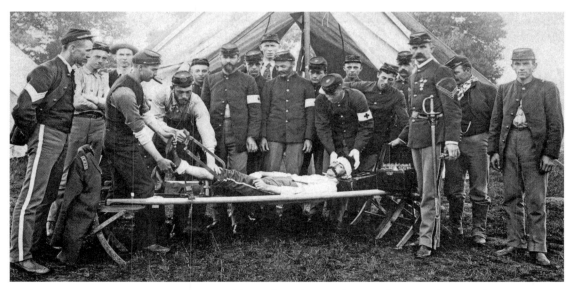

A doctor prepares to amputate a soldier's leg during the Civil War. Those who survived such surgery faced a high risk of infection, because most doctors didn't wash their hands or equipment before performing surgery. It wasn't until the late 1800s that doctors understood the importance of cleanliness in the operating room.

Dr. Williams kept the area where he did surgery spotless, whether it was in his office or in a patient's home. He often scrubbed the walls, floor, and ceilings of an operating area himself to kill as many germs as possible. As a result, hardly any of his patients got infections. Dr. Williams's patients liked him so much they started calling him Dr. Dan. The nickname stayed with him for the rest of his life.

This photo shows Provident Hospital in the 1890s, as well as Dr. Williams and two of the hospital's nursing students. At Provident, Dr. Williams started the first training school for black nurses in the United States.

Dr. Williams became known in Chicago as an excellent surgeon. Yet despite his reputation, he had a hard time getting any of his African American patients into Chicago hospitals when they needed additional treatment. This is when he decided to start up a new hospital, one that would train black nurses, hire black doctors, and welcome all patients, regardless of color. Dr. Williams's hospital—which he named Provident Hospital—opened in 1891.

Under Dr. Williams's supervision, Provident had a super-successful first year. In those days, most people who ended up in a hospital died, usually from bacterial infections. In Provident's first year, out of 189 patients, 167 improved or recovered completely. Only 22 patients died.

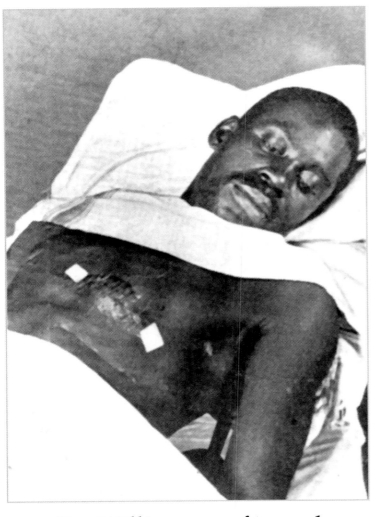

Daniel Hale Williams was one of the earliest doctors to perform successful surgery around the heart. His patient, James Cornish, is shown here recovering after the operation in 1893.

In 1893, two years after Provident Hospital opened, Dr. Williams performed an extraordinary operation. A patient named James Cornish was brought to the hospital. He had been stabbed in the chest during a knife fight and was dying. Dr. Williams suspected his patient's heart had been pierced, and prepared to operate. At this time, there were no X-ray machines, **blood transfusions,** or bacteria-fighting drugs.

Opening a person's chest to see if the heart was damaged was almost unheard of at the time, and was extremely risky. But Dr. Williams felt confident. He had a staff of excellent doctors and nurses to assist him.

Dr. Williams began the operation. He found James Cornish's heart was just slightly pierced, but the **pericardium,** the protective sac that surrounds the heart, was seriously damaged. Dr. Williams successfully repaired the pericardium and stitched up Cornish's chest. The operation saved his patient's life!

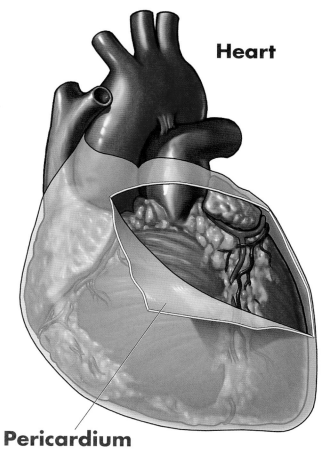

Heart

Pericardium

This illustration of a human heart shows the pericardium, the protective sac around the heart. Dr. Williams successfully repaired James Cornish's pericardium.

Newspapers across the United States quickly spread the news of Dr. Williams's successful operation. Suddenly, Daniel Hale Williams was famous throughout the world. In 1893, he received an invitation to come to Washington, D.C., and make improvements to a hospital there. Freedmen's Hospital, which had been founded to treat former slaves during the Civil War, was seriously run-down. It needed someone like Dr. Daniel Hale Williams to help get it in shape.

Dr. Williams took on the challenge. When he arrived at Freedmen's Hospital, he found patients crammed together in filthy, insect-infested rooms. Right away, he fired poorly performing doctors and replaced them with skilled, hardworking ones. He retrained nurses and got everyone to clean the place so it was spotless.

After four years of hard work, Daniel Hale Williams had turned things completely around at Freedmen's Hospital, which later became Howard University Hospital. Before he arrived there, Freedmen's was known as a place where patients rarely recovered. Now, thanks to Dr. Williams, it was a hospital where patients could expect to be cured. Because he wanted people to know how much Freedmen's had improved, Dr. Williams even invited the public to stop by every Sunday to watch him perform surgery in the operating room.

In 1898, Dr. Williams married Alice Johnson.

Fixing Freedmen's Hospital wasn't the only thing Daniel Hale Williams accomplished in Washington, D.C. He also fell in love and got married while he was there. Dr. Williams met his future wife at a party. They got along really well. After dating for six months, Daniel Hale Williams and Alice Johnson got married. Soon after the wedding, the couple headed to Chicago, where Dr. Williams returned to Provident Hospital.

Even though Daniel Hale Williams had brought great improvements to Freedmen's Hospital, some people there didn't appreciate him. The head surgeon he replaced never forgave Dr. Williams for taking his job. Some jealous doctors started false rumors that Dr. Williams was misusing the hospital's money.

When Daniel Hale Williams got back to Provident, he found that some doctors and hospital officials there wanted to run things their own way. These people gave him a hard time, too. Dr. Williams was disappointed, especially since some of the people working against him were old friends.

Dr. Williams (seated in chair) with some of his nursing students at Freedmen's Hospital

Dr. Williams never had the patience to defend himself against complaints and made-up rumors. He preferred to spend his time and energy on curing patients and helping educate doctors and nurses. In 1912, a fed-up Dr. Williams decided to leave Provident, the hospital he had founded.

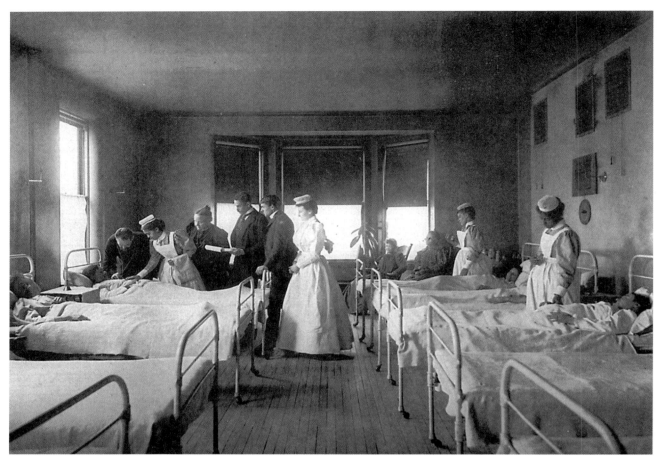

Dr. Williams (standing, fourth from left) in a ward at Provident Hospital

After he left Provident Hospital, Dr. Williams kept as busy as ever. He was invited to work at other hospitals around the country as a surgeon and teacher. In 1920, he and his wife built a retirement home in the woods of northern Michigan. Dr. Williams was now able to enjoy his favorite activities: hunting, fishing, and swimming.

Dr. Williams died in 1931 at his home in Idlewild, Michigan. He had been among the first surgeons to operate successfully on the area surrounding the human heart. Today, the thirteen-bed hospital he founded in 1891 is a large, modern medical center. Daniel Hale Williams opened the doors of medicine to African Americans, and his career continues to inspire many people long after his death.

Daniel Hale Williams enjoying a quiet moment in his study

Glossary

amputate (AM-pyuh-tate) To cut off a part of the body, usually because it is damaged or diseased

anesthesia (AN-us-THEE-zhuh) A drug or gas given to a patient so that they do not feel pain during surgery

antiseptic (an-tih-SEP-tik) A substance that kills and prevents the growth of disease-causing germs

apprentice (uh-PREN-tiss) A person who learns a trade by working under the supervision of a skilled person

bacteria (bak-TIHR-ee-uh) Microscopic organisms, some of which cause disease

blood transfusion (BLUHD transs-FYOO-zhuhn) The injection of blood from one person into the body of someone else who needs blood because of injury or illness

germ (JURM) A very small living organism that can cause disease

infection (in-FEK-shuhn) An illness caused by germs or viruses

non-segregated (NON-SEG-ruh-gay-tid) Not kept apart on the basis of race

pericardium (per-ih-CAR-dee-uhm) The sac that surrounds the human heart

racial prejudice (RAY-shuhl PREJ-uh-diss) Hatred or unfair treatment of people because of the color of their skin

sterile (STER-uhl) Free from germs and dirt

Index